Douglas, Debbie D.
Now what? 12 strategies to
landing the career you'll love
2023.
39305258317571
bk   07/03/24

☐ SO-EKI-066

Now What?

12 Strategies to Landing the Career You'll Love, Not Tolerate

Debbie D. Douglas

© 2023 by Debbie D. Douglas

ALL RIGHTS RESERVED.

Published in the United States by Pen Legacy Publishing
An imprint of Pen Legacy, LLC, Pennsylvania
www.penlegacy.com

Library of Congress Cataloging – in- Publication Data has been
applied for.

Paperback ISBN: 979-8-9891638-7-8
eBook ISBN: 979-8-9872891-7-4

Editing & Formatting by: Carla M. Dean, U Can Mark My Word
Book Cover Design by: Christian Cuan

PRINTED IN THE UNITED STATES OF AMERICA.

Table of Contents

Now What?

12 Strategies to Landing the Career
You'll Love, Not Tolerate

Welcome

Congratulations on your collegiate graduation! Congratulations on taking the next step in your career! Congratulations on making the choice to finally choose *you*!

Despite the devastation of the coronavirus that affected people worldwide and the financial woes many experienced due to the pandemic, Americans became more motivated than ever to make life-altering decisions regarding their careers, retirement, relocation, travel, or homeownership. The old philosophy of "staying in a job you hate but are grateful to have" has changed to "if it's not making you happy, leave." If you are reading this book, I think it is safe to assume you are among the 95% committed to finding the answers that will propel you forward in your career, and I am ready to help you.

Debbie D. Douglas

Before we get started, allow me to introduce myself. I am Debbie D. Douglas, a career coach and human resources recruiter. My human resources career began over twenty years ago within Talent Acquisition at Paramount (formerly MTV Networks). From there, I acquired talent for Paramount (BET Networks), Ketchum, worked in PR/Communications for an Omnicom company, and then returned to Paramount (formerly Viacom CBS) in 2013. In my various positions, I am usually the first point of contact for a potential candidate after applying.

Although my experience has been primarily in television and cable recruitment, the mindset and checklist, as it pertains to the recruitment process, are the same. For example, in every industry, when a job seeker applies for a job, they must undergo the standard hiring process of a résumé critique, job interview, and reference checks. The only part of the process that is always different is the recruiter ensuring that the potential candidate has the required experience, skills, and education to perform satisfactorily. That's where I come in. I will help you understand what recruiters are looking for within the hiring process and provide you with the tools and strategies so that you will be prepared, organized, and aligned to receive the offer letter.

Now What?

If you are ready to land the career you'll love and not just tolerate—which I'm sure you are because why else would you be reading this book, then dive into these strategies so you can implement, execute, and win big! I am rooting for you!

Before Applying for Jobs, Do This...

There are a few things a job seeker can control during their job search. Choosing which job to apply for is one of them. The positions you choose to apply for should be calculated and focused. Applying for every job on a company's career site will get you labeled a "serial applier." Trust me, you do not want to be a serial applicant. Be discerning about the roles you apply for within a company. To do that, here are a few questions to consider that will help get you closer to landing the desired job that will lead to career success.

- What kind of position are you seeking? Do you meet the basic qualifications for that role?
- Where is the job located? Are you willing to relocate?
- What industry are you interested in working in? Do you have experience, education, or transferrable skills?
- When can you start? Are you prepared to start within a few weeks or require a three-to-six-month plan?
- What is your job search strategy? Do you have a coach, or are you working with a recruitment agency?
- Do you have a person who works in that industry with whom you can discuss the position or company culture?
- What are your salary requirements? Are you willing to negotiate?
- Is your job search driven by money alone?
- Do you have a side business? If so, is there a possibility it may hinder you from carrying out your responsibilities in the new job?

When preparing for your job-seeking journey, being clear about what you want will help narrow the search. In addition, it will prevent you from applying for a position for which you do not qualify.

As a recruiter, please remember we are rating your résumé on your ability to perform the job. Thus, your résumé and the job description must align. So, I implore you to consider these questions prior to starting your job search. Take time to think and answer honestly, and be confident about your answers. Once you know what you want, and the recruiter sees you as the "perfect fit" to their organization's puzzle, you will move on to the next phase—the interview. To further help you, here are a few tips you might not know:

- Employers can tell how prepared you are and how much you know about the industry/company from how your résumé is structured.
- Do you show signs of being a "flight risk"? In an effort to avoid having a high turnover rate within the company, recruiters are hyper-focused on learning how you will fit into the company's short-term and long-term plans.
- Employers want to know that you will be a loyal employee open to learning, being an asset, and growing with the company.

Strategy 1
What Feeds Your P.A.P.
(Passion and Pockets)?

When I was younger, I was timid and rarely spoke up out of fear of sounding unintelligent, especially at school. Yet, when surrounded by family and friends, I would light up and was usually the center of attention. I guess you can say I felt comfortable around people I knew and those who loved me. However, while taking courses to complete my Social Work major, another side to me was born. The majority of our assignments were required to be given in presentation format. After a while of participating in group work and speaking in front of the class, you couldn't get me to be quiet. Those classes helped me evolve into a woman with a bold voice who had something to say. I learned to control the room and had a way of making people feel whatever emotion I was projecting as I spoke. To master this skill, I volunteered for any opportunity that would allow me to practice to perfection speaking in front of groups of people.

What skill do you need to master? Does your dream job require you to step outside of your comfort zone? Once I knew that a career in Human Resources was my goal, I stepped into my role and became better. When identifying your passion and purpose, ensure that your dream job matches. For instance, many of us may have dreamed of becoming a doctor, knowing we hate math and science. Are you willing to compromise and study those subjects to pursue your passion? Once I discovered my love of communicating, landing a job where I corresponded for a living became necessary. And when it comes to the recruiting process, recruiters are looking for candidates who are passionate about the job, the industry, the mission, and the purpose. Are you excited about the company's mission? How does that mission align with your personal mission? As a recruiter, we want to ensure you are as committed to coming to work as we are! Make sure you speak to this on your résumé. The following are a few more things for you to consider:

- What activities or hobbies excite you or motivate you? Are they aligned with your dream job or the career you are applying for?
- What are you good at and derive joy from doing? What makes you happy with little to no effort?
- Do you like working from behind a desk, or would you prefer a job where you are outdoors, working with your hands, or doing physical labor?
- Are you comfortable taking directions from others, or would you rather be an entrepreneur?

Strategy 2
Research the Field of Your Interest

C ongratulations! You've made it to the interview! I will bet you are excited, and the recruiter welcomes the opportunity to learn more about you. However, please understand that even though you have reached this level, this is not the time to slack. You must bring your A-game. The interview is your one chance to make an impression by pitching your desires, expressing your understanding of what the company does, and explaining how you will solve the company's problem(s) and add value to the department's culture. Understanding what the company does is essential because knowing this will help solidify your chances of landing your dream job. This is where the majority of applicants trip up and lose the race. Think of it this way, how can you ask to be a part of a company, marketplace, or industry without understanding the history, services, leadership, mission, values, and the overall idea of what they do and who they represent? Most employers seek individuals who align with and understand the nature of the company. It's just like joining a professional or personal organization. How many of you are joining without first doing your research? In other words, joining just to belong!

When it comes to recruiters, it is our job to ensure we know you and that you know us. Our job is not to teach you the things you should already know or ignore your limited knowledge about the company or position just because you will get an overview during orientation. You have to show up ready!

So, as you start your research, here are some questions I suggest you ask yourself:

- What about this company makes you want to be employed with them?
- Why are you interested in that particular role? Are you experienced?
- What is the company's mission, and how do you align?
- What are the founding principles, and how do they show up in your life?

- What skills and/or talents does the position require?
- What are three things that intrigue you about the company? Are you a supporter of the brand?
- What formal education or certificates and licenses are needed, if any?
- What are the pay ranges for starting positions in your field of interest? Does that satisfy your financial need?
- Is the industry growing or declining?
- Do you have the time and/or resources to enroll in college or any formal educational program to gain additional education, if necessary?
- Are you willing to take a pay cut to gain entry into that company?

To clarify, coming to an interview without knowing the basic information is as bad as having a résumé full of typographical errors. As a recruiter, it disappoints me when applicants can't answer the question, *Why do you want to work for our company?* When a person can't answer that question during the interview, it gives me the impression that their sole focus is to land *any* job, regardless of the position, and get paid. Now before you give me the eye-roll, I understand salary is essential. However, from a recruiter's standpoint, your response to that question helps us align you with the company, see your value, and appreciate your readiness. Your goal is to confirm the confidence within the recruiter and hiring manager in your capabilities and their faith that you will be a vital asset. Nobody wants to invest their time in hiring and training an employee only to learn the person is a flight risk or a poor performer.

Check out *The Occupational Outlook Handbook* online for resources to assist in your research.

Strategy 3
Choose Companies That Align with Your Interests, Values, and Trajectory

E mployers and recruiters alike can tell if you are genuinely interested in the company and the position or just looking for a paycheck. The best way to set yourself up for the win is to avoid showcasing that your interest, values, or trajectory *do not* align. I am not saying you must be in complete unison with a company. That would be unrealistic. However, ensure you can relate to, have a genuine concern for, or be passionate about what they do and who they serve. How would you feel if your physician treated you without any care about your well-being? They just prescribe you medication and send you on your way without listening to your concerns! How would you feel? Dismissed? Annoyed? Ready to place a call to the State medical board? Or would you likely start looking for a new physician? Exactly!

As previously stated, I've worked in the media and entertainment industry for the better part of my career. At one point, a recruiter within a public relations/communications agency contacted me regarding an opportunity, and out of haste, I took a chance. At first, I was excited about the opportunity because it was NEW, offered a chance to expand my existing management skills, and provided more independence while also offering the ability to partner with the executive team. Only focusing on the positives of the position, I failed to research whether the company aligned with my interests, values, and trajectory. At the time, I was more concerned about the growth opportunity and less about the big picture. So here I was in a new industry, flopping around like a fish out of water.

- I didn't feel as though I belonged.
- I was one of the few diverse faces in the office, which is another issue in and of itself.
- I didn't feel like I was on equal footing as others, given I had to learn a new industry and do it in an environment where I didn't feel fully seen.

- I realized the work wasn't exciting, and I lacked the enthusiasm I once had in my past company.

This is why it is important to research your industry and make sure you are aligned with the company, department, culture, and diversity mindset. Ignoring this critical work can impact your career journey by causing unnecessary stress, delayed goals, involuntary termination, or the personal need to resign.

As you research the industries, pick at least five to ten companies that resonate with your career trajectory. Now list the characteristics that most interest you and assess the companies based on your research.

Here are some questions to answer as you complete this strategy:

- What is the corporate culture?
- Can you get behind and believe in the company's product(s) or service(s)? Does it excite you? Can you relate to the business?
- Do they have a diverse and inclusive workforce?
- Do they invest in their employees' growth?
- Do they have a history of giving back to the community?

These are just a few factors to consider as you narrow down the right company.

The following are several great resources to assist you in seeking helpful information regarding your companies of interest:

- Glassdoor
- Fishbowl
- LinkedIn
- Company's website
- Company's social media pages (Instagram, Facebook, YouTube, Snapchat, TikTok, Twitter, etc.)

Strategy 4
How to Get Recruiters & Employers Knocking Down Your Door with the Perfect Résumé

I f you are like many individuals, crafting the perfect résumé is a grueling experience. I mean, what all is supposed to be included in it? A recruiter will tell you to keep it one to two pages, your friend will say don't add the professional summary, and your co-worker will suggest putting everything (selling yourself). When creating a résumé, this is your chance to sell yourself. It's almost like marketing and pitching. Think about it this way—your résumé is your way of trying to convince, persuade, and sell your experience, education, volunteer service, and professional outlook to people you don't know in hopes they will see your value and worth. Daunting, I know. However, you can make this experience lighter just by tailoring your résumé.

Google offers great résumé templates for various industries. It will also show you what elements need to be in the résumé so you structure it accordingly. Once you are done creating your résumé, make sure to hire a proofreader, editor, or someone who is qualified in writing to review your résumé for grammatical, punctuation, spelling, spacing, font, and developmental errors. You would be surprised how many résumés land in my company's database that are filled with errors, incomplete, have cover letters addressed to our competitors, etc. A surefire way NOT to get called for an interview is not taking extra precautions before submitting your résumé. In addition to what was already stated, here are some more basic tips:

- What does your résumé say about you?
- Are you struggling with how to make sure your résumé stands out?
- Know your audience (employer) and tailor your résumé to align with them.
- Tailor your résumé to highlight your relevant and transferable skills. (Reference keywords mentioned in the job description that align with your experience.)

- Highlight your accomplishments for every job, no matter how big or small.

- Keep your résumé at one to two pages at the most for entry-level positions and recent graduates, unless you are a senior-level, executive, or seeking federal employment. *Note: In some cases, it could be longer, depending on the field. For example, the production staff I hire usually add their credits of TV shows they have worked on, which is customary in the TV/Entertainment space.*

- Tailor your résumé to the job for which you are applying. It's okay to have more than one version of your résumé that plays to the strengths of each role and company you are applying for.

- Add a link to your LinkedIn profile, professional website, or portfolio if you have one.

- Take off irrelevant jobs or internships, especially if it's not aligned with the jobs you're gunning for as of present. (This is more specific to early career professionals who have already had one to two jobs out of college, not specifically recent college graduates with limited work/volunteer experience.)

- Cover letters are unique to the job, industry, and recruiter. If it's asked of you, include one. If not, don't feel compelled to write one unless you must elaborate on gaps in your employment, making a career transition, etc.

- Always include your tangible skills, i.e., software, programs, special technical skills, etc.
- Don't forget to think outside the box and use your creativity.

Be creative! Let's touch on that one for a second. I recall when a candidate mailed a cake to our offices with his résumé printed on top! Not only was it unexpected, but the candidate was applying for an accountant role, which most stereotypes assume has a type A personality and isn't very creative. With this action, he found a way to stand out in a creative industry, although his role was not. He did not allow his profession to define him. Yes, this was over the top, and no, we don't expect anyone to send us résumé topped cakes. However, do not be afraid to put a unique stamp on your résumé or any correspondence you may submit to the company leading up to the interview. That candidate's effort and creativity went a long way, and I still have that memory imprinted in my mind.

Another example I recall is when a candidate sent a résumé formatted as a press announcement, and they were seeking a marketing/PR role. It showed they were knowledgeable, innovative, and passionate about the field while putting a fun spin on it. It's okay to be creative, so go ahead and get those creative juices flowing! Somebody is waiting for your résumé!

Strategy 5
Give Your Social Media & Professional Brand a Tune-Up... or Establish One

I have always been of the mindset that social media is only for "social" purposes! However, as society has evolved, social media has taken center stage when building brands, businesses, networks, and showcasing skills, services, products, and even ourselves. Recently, employers joined social media platforms to share job vacancies, view potential candidates, and assess your portfolio for character identification. Business News Daily (Cotriss, 2023) noted, "*Make sure your social media profiles are safe for work because employers are screening candidates' presence online.*

Debbie D. Douglas

Generally, employers are looking for any red flags. These could include the sharing of illegal activities, offensive comments, violent or aggressive behavior, sexually explicit material, or confidential information. Some of the platforms they are likely to check are LinkedIn, Instagram, Facebook, Twitter, TikTok, and WhatsApp."

With this in mind, it's time to clean up or properly position your social media to reflect the best version of you. For me, this has caused me to let go of the notion that social media is my private space dedicated to only family and friends. When coworkers would ask me if I had social media or wanted to connect, I would nicely decline. At the time, I believed we shouldn't mix business with pleasure. There are boundaries!

In a recent article by *Forbes*, "The Power of Social Media in Recruiting," Niki Jorgensen emphasized that we (employers/recruiters) need to develop more brand awareness for our companies. *"Social media remains underutilized in recruiting, so in 2023, businesses should leverage social media to recruit the best candidates and establish a pipeline for the future."*

Thus, as much as we may feel like it's all an invasion of privacy, social media is a part of the hiring process. Recruiters and hiring managers are on all platforms trying to bridge the gaps and meet you where you are. Think about it; if recruiters are interested in learning more about you within your "personal" space, use it to your advantage. Showcase your skills, give proof that you are already doing the job, add value to what you are doing in your community, and shine like the most qualified candidate possible. Don't miss out on using your social media brand as a direct tactic to be seen and chosen by employers.

You may be asking, "Debbie, how can I effectively integrate social media into my job search strategy?" Quick answer: Utilize your social media accounts to highlight your passion, experience, interests, and expertise in the industries you are interested in. Have no idea where or how to begin? There are a multitude of ways in which you can capitalize on your existing profiles. Let's take LinkedIn for example:

- LinkedIn: a professional networking platform where you can create a unique career profile. We'll refer to it as an interactive résumé. You can display more of your professional personality here.
- Join niche professional groups that exist on LinkedIn and other professional platforms. Leverage the tools on these sites to interact with like-minded professionals, network, and stay relevant online. Usually, these online groups have chat forums, job postings, or other relevant ways to interact with professionals, including

recruiters like myself, who are looking for you! Yes, we join professional groups to recruit talent all the time.

- Add websites, a portfolio, or links to your work. (This is particularly important for creatives but is not limited to these professionals.)
- Add documents, presentations, or reports you've completed and want to highlight.
- Highlight awards, volunteer work, or leadership positions.
- Upload videos that showcase examples of your work or related content you've created for your current employer. (Absolutely NO proprietary information should be included.)

Content is king in the entertainment, television, streaming, and cable industries. Think about every opportunity to use your content to showcase your skills and knowledge.

These are the primary areas you can utilize to stay relevant. There are a lot of runways to work with to get your "personal and professional" brand garnering your desired attention. Don't limit yourself! You don't have to be a creative to think creatively. As mentioned earlier, recruiters are meeting talent where they are, and that includes on social media platforms of all forms.

Strategy 6
Identifying Your Ideal Job

What is your ideal job? A perfect job is one where you feel satisfied and look forward to going to work. Now, it's important to note that an ideal job differs for everyone. You may define your perfect job as one where you serve others, while someone else defines their perfect job as one with a short commute and good pay. Knowing what you want from your job is essential during this entire process because it answers the question: "What do you want to do that will maintain your sanity and level of happiness or bring you happiness?" So, before we continue, take a minute to think about that. What do you want from your job?

Debbie D. Douglas

Having total clarity and confirmation regarding your ideal job will allow you the ability to screen employers and job descriptions properly and decide what you are willing to accept, compromise for, or flat-out deny. Moreover, this will help you not waste the recruiter's time reviewing, responding, or processing your job request. Let's do the opposite and maximize your and the recruiter's time. Not having clarity in your ideal job creates a disconnect between you and the recruiter, ultimately leading to no calls. I have had people share their lack of belief in the hiring process and that recruiters aren't calling, and I always have to explain that there is more to it than what meets the eye. There are many factors that lead to candidates being overlooked or declined for interviews—some with no fault of the candidate. However, allow me to mitigate a few of the red flags you have control of.

- Take a step back to think whether your résumé would stand out amongst other qualified applicants.
- Would you consider yourself a Subject Matter Expert (SME) in the position advertised?
- Do you check off at least 85% of the required qualifications listed or relevant, tangible transferable skills?

Do some self-inventory of your skills and match them up with the description. Focus only on those jobs, and apply to a targeted list of roles and companies that speak to your ideal job. Because I am a "cool" recruiter, here are a few methods you can use to help you land the career you'll love, not tolerate.

- Identify the dream companies you want to work for.
- Develop mentorships with those in your desired field.
- Take a personality test to gauge your interests.
- Be proactive with companies you want to work for by volunteering or participating in exterior opportunities.
- Take advantage of internship opportunities.
- Talk with a career counselor or consultant.
- Pursue additional volunteer work in another department at your current company to gain experience.

Strategy 7
Are You Ready to Apply?

When I prepare for a trip, I create a to-do list to ensure I accomplish everything needed leading up to when it's time for me to check in for my flight. I put together my outfits for how many days I'll be traveling, including the one I will fly out in and my return flight outfit. I put together all the accessories that will complement each outfit. I pay attention to what type of activities I'll participate in and keep that in mind when planning my outfits. I ensure I have enough cash, download my boarding pass, and make sure I have my ID and passport. So, where am I going with this? I'm glad you asked. The same way we "ready ourselves" for dates, trips, or events we attend, we need to "ready ourselves" for the job market as competitive candidates. Although we discussed a few strategies to ensure you are ready, the following are simple yet critical items that should always be a part of your formal job application. You would be surprised how many applicants don't have these buttoned up when applying for jobs.

First things first, set up a candidate profile on all the company career sites and independent job sites where you are interested in pursuing opportunities. What does this entail? Here are the basic details you'll need to create your profile. This section may be more of a refresher if you are a seasoned professional.

- Upload personal information and contact information.
- Upload a résumé or information about current and past jobs. Some career sites allow you to upload your résumé directly; others require you to fill it out per job until all the pertinent information is included. Include salary requirements, ideally your minimum average. (You can refer to the job postings for the median range depending on the state where you live.)

Pro Tip: In the State of New York, we are mandated to disclose the salary averages on all job postings as of the last quarter of 2022. You can look up your state to see if they must disclose your area's median range. (Pay Transparency Laws by State [2023] – Zippia)

- Choose departments and titles that align with your experience and passion. Decide how often you want to receive job alerts. You can always update your preferences at a later date in the event your interests shift.
- Add a portfolio or samples of your work. Samples can be anything from projects, deliverables, or career highlights to attract more eyeballs and prospective employers.
- Ensure your LinkedIn profile or other professional profile/bio is updated. Recruiters make lists of prospective candidates using LinkedIn and other relevant platforms to curate searches.
- Cover letters are usually industry-specific. Thus they are not always required. However, it's nice to have one. They become more relevant if you are in a career transition, have gaps in your résumé, or want to provide more information your résumé doesn't reveal.

- Ensure you can accommodate interview requests. Flexibility is key! When you apply for a job, flexibility around interviewing times is mandatory. The same applies to the recruiting/hiring team. They should also be flexible when scheduling candidates, especially if the candidate is currently employed.
- Make sure your email address and contact number on your résumé are accurate. Clear out your voicemail or set up a voicemail if you don't have one.
- Make sure your email name is appropriate to include on a résumé.

All the aforementioned details matter!

Strategy 8
Be Realistic and Flexible

B e realistic and flexible with what you've envisioned for your career. Be flexible with salary requirements and growth potential if the role shows opportunities for advancement. To reach your final destination, are you willing to accept a junior-level position that provides room for professional development and learning that may be required for the desired promotion? For example, many recent graduates I've interviewed come to the table expecting top salaries by applying for positions that do not match their experience and tenure.

A word to the wise, if you are a recent graduate,

Debbie D. Douglas

applying for an entry, assistant, or coordinator position is your best bet. These positions typically lay the foundation and required skills needed to perform in your analyst or middle management roles by developing strong professional communication, administrative, organization, and multi-tasking skills. It sets the framework for learning the industry, the key players, and the trajectory for your desired career track. Let's be clear, though. Not every career journey follows a straight path to the top. We often end up making lateral-type moves or take a few steps back to go five steps forward.

Pro Tip: Scrap the idea that the title, role, and company have to be exactly what you THINK you want! Focus on the long-term goals. Sometimes skills you obtain from other positions can help you gain access to your future role and supply a great foundation for that dream role!

Strategy 9
Interview Hacks 101

Y ou made it! Even though we have touched on interviewing previously, I want to offer some tips to guarantee you stand out and leave a great impression.

- Arrive at least fifteen minutes early if your interview is in person. This allows you time for a quick wardrobe check or bathroom break. If your interview is online, check your Zoom or whatever video platform will be utilized at least five minutes prior to the start of the interview—if not earlier—to ensure there are no technical issues with the video, audio, or connecting to Wi-Fi. Remember, arriving on time is actually late!

- Keep your wardrobe simple and professional. Even though "professional attire" varies now, you still want to be as close to standard as possible.

- For men, you can't go wrong with collared shirt and slacks or a suit if it's a conservative corporate setting.

- For women, proper attire is a suitable length skirt coupled with a blazer and blouse or a workplace dress. Avoid blouses with plunging necklines or leaving too many top buttons undone. Your cleavage doesn't need to be the center of attention.

- Wearing sneakers or flip-flops to an interview is a no-no. Your clothes and shoes should not distract the interviewer from focusing on learning more about you through your personality and skills.

- Be authentically you! Don't try to portray yourself as something or someone you are not! If you must do that to prove yourself, then you're probably not interviewing at the right company.

- Never speak negatively about your current or former employer if you have experienced an unpleasant situation. Speak about what you learned in the situation and how you overcame challenges, and express that you are looking for opportunities that align with your work style, management, etc. Find the positive even in a negative situation.

- The receptionist, admin, or coordinators you interact with are also paying attention. Be courteous and professional with them, as well. You would be surprised what we learn from them when they have unpleasant interactions with rude applicants.

- Use the job description as a basic frame for your questions. Use the information the recruiter shares to build on other impromptu questions. NEVER leave without asking questions. If you have no questions, the recruiter assumes you think you know all there is to know about the position, which is definitely not the case.

- Eye contact is important, whether in person or online. This shows you are engaged and interested in what the recruiter has to say.

- Keep your body language in check. Sit up straight, no slouching. Lean in when listening to show you are interested in what you are hearing.

- Be prepared to have examples of big wins and learning moments.

- Give examples of how you will be an asset to the company or department and processes you will be able to improve based on the information provided to you.

- Be able to speak about areas you can improve on. Nobody is perfect. When they ask about your weaknesses, be honest. Share what you would like to continue to build on to become better. It shows you are human and a work in process. We all are!

For more information, refer to the following link: as a quick reference for common job interview questions. This will help you prepare for the interviews:

→   https://hbr.org/2021/11/10-common-job-interview-questions-and-how-to-answer-them

Strategy 10
You Made It Through the Interview. Now What?

A t this point in the recruiting process, as the candidate, you want to leave an impression and stay relevant as the hiring team continues to meet with other applicants. The best way to do this is to keep the lines of communication open and stay top of mind! Within 24-48 hours after your interview, you should do the following:

- Send a "Thank You" note to all interviewers. Ensure you personalize each message. NEVER copy and paste a thank you note. Keep in mind that most interview teams and hiring departments share notes. You want to come across as a serious candidate who took something special or unique away from each meeting. Also, don't forget to check your grammar! Sending a thank you note with grammatical errors will leave a bad image of you to those who interviewed you and possibly jeopardize your chances of being hired.

- Send any additional items that may aid in your candidate's consideration. Samples of your work or examples of how you can add value to the role based on the knowledge you received in the interview are great ways to be seen as a memorable candidate who was vested in the interview process.
- Reiterate your passion for the job and why you should be considered a competitive candidate.

These are just a few tips to help you impress upon the company your intent to be chosen as a final candidate and land in the career you'll LOVE, not tolerate!

Strategy 11
Congratulations!
You've Received an Offer(s)!

Well done! I am super proud of you. I know I offered you a lot of strategies, tips, and tools that you've applied and executed to get to this point, but now what? What questions should you ask? It's so much to reflect on before you accept. One thing is, don't accept the first offer. Always negotiate salary unless that conversation is had in advance of the offer. Salary can vary by the type of role, industry, and levels. Share your justification as to why your experience calls for your ideal salary.

Research the comp levels—average and your state's

averages—by industry. Every industry is different and pays on a different scale. As mentioned earlier, states now disclose salary averages in their job postings. This helps to mitigate any confusion and manages expectations on the employer and prospective employee's part. Don't be unrealistic about the salary. What does this mean? Let's explore the following to ensure this offer is the offer for you:

- Are the health benefits suitable for you, your family, your spouse, etc.?
- What are the culture and diversity strategies? Does it align with what is important to you? Remember that some non-monetary benefits can equate to monetary benefits overall, so the total package is what you should be focused on. When you receive an offer, you'll want to negotiate your salary if it does not meet your minimum requirements.
- What rewards and benefits mean the most to you? In today's employment market, compensation is not the only motivating factor that makes for an attractive offer.
- Is there a remote, hybrid, or in-person requirement? What are your deal breakers, and what are the pros and cons?

- Is the paid time off sufficient for your lifestyle? Take into consideration what is realistic and what isn't. For example, do you travel often? Do you have to call out often because you take care of a parent or a young child? (This would be more relevant for those who are not single, have aging parents, or have a pre-existing condition that may cause you to call out more than the average employee.)
- Does the company offer tuition reimbursement? Are you currently in school or plan to continue your education? Think about how these factors can affect your household budget and personal finances. Benefits like these can take the place of a higher base salary and ultimately help you secure a promotion or salary increase eventually.

Your total "rewards" are not all in the form of a monetary benefit but can improve your overall package, resulting in a long-term financial benefit. Never forget that!

Strategy 12
Congratulations!
You've Landed the Career
of Your Dreams!

I will leave you with some essential tips to help you make the most of your new job and company:

- Request any organizational charts, departmental standard operating procedure (SOP), departmental policies, processes, or job-related reading material that can help you get acclimated to the team, goals, and expectations.
- Set up individual meetings/lunches during your first two weeks with team members and other

internal stakeholders with whom you will directly collaborate. Developing a good rapport and strong partnership with your teammates benefits you, the team, and the company!

Strategy Session

As you embark on the journey outlined in *Now What? 12 Strategies to Landing the Career You'll Love, Not Tolerate*, it's crucial to remember that change is the cornerstone of growth and success. Whether you're a recent college graduate or a seasoned professional seeking to pivot your career, this book is designed to guide you through the transition with tried-and-true practical strategies I've utilized and recommend.

Before we part, I want you to begin your journey with a clear vision and an open mindset. The action item now that you've completed this book is to set aside some time to truly envision your ideal career. Reflect on your passions, strengths, and the impact you want to make. Start to tackle each of these strategies, and jot down your career goals no matter how ambitious they may seem. This is the first step toward creating a fulfilling and purpose-driven career path.

Passions:

_____

_____

_____

_____

_____

_____

_____

_____

_____

_____

_____

_____

_____

_____

_____

Strengths:

_____

_____

_____

_____

_____

_____

_____

_____

_____

_____

_____

_____

_____

_____

_____

_____

_____

_____

Debbie D. Douglas

What is your desired impact over the next year?

_____

_____

_____

_____

_____

_____

_____

_____

_____

_____

_____

_____

_____

_____

_____

_____

_____

_____

What do your desired career goals look like and what steps will you take to accomplish them? Write them down and visualize it.

_____

_____

_____

_____

_____

_____

_____

_____

_____

_____

_____

_____

_____

_____

_____

_____

Debbie D. Douglas

<u>Create Timelines</u>

30-day goal:

_____

_____

_____

_____

_____

_____

_____

_____

_____

_____

_____

_____

_____

_____

_____

_____

_____

90-day goal:

_____

_____

_____

_____

_____

_____

_____

_____

_____

_____

_____

_____

_____

_____

_____

_____

_____

_____

Debbie D. Douglas

120-day goal:

_____

_____

_____

_____

_____

_____

_____

_____

_____

_____

_____

_____

_____

_____

_____

_____

_____

_____

About The Author

D ebbie Douglas is a Brooklyn, NY, native currently living in New Jersey. Debbie began her HR career as an HR Assistant at the Shubert Organization, a unionized theatrical management company in NY, home to Broadway theaters across the U.S. She later joined the HR department at Paramount, formerly MTV Networks, a global media & entertainment conglomerate. Debbie worked her way up from Assistant in Talent Acquisition and was eventually promoted to Recruiter/TA Manager. In that capacity, she managed the recruitment process from start to finish—from sourcing candidates to negotiating job offers. She also stepped out of her comfort zone and explored other opportunities throughout her career.

Debbie spent time at Alloy Media + Marketing. At the time, Alloy was known as a non-traditional youth and media marketing company. In this role, she shifted from sole recruitment to working as an HR Manager/Generalist. Her main focus was employee relations, recruitment, and training/facilitation. In addition to recruitment, she supported various functions of performance management, compensation, and benefits. In her time with the company, she formalized their job posting process, established their first AAP (Affirmative Action Plan), and assisted in negotiating with the vendor for their first-ever ATS, Applicant Tracking System.

Debbie inevitably returned to Paramount as Senior HR Manager of Human Resources and Talent Management at BET Networks. As one of the dedicated staffing resources professionals, she focused on full-cycle recruitment and new hire onboarding, with dedicated support in management training and employee programs. From there, she had a short stint at a global public relations & communications company, Ketchum, as a senior recruiter overseeing a small team in the NY office. She recruited for all senior-level hires across the agency and offices in DC, Chicago, and LA.

Her passion for media and entertainment was too much of a draw for her to stay within the agency setting. So, she returned to Paramount, where she recruited for all the brands under the Paramount portfolio across various creative functions. Debbie currently sits in the Director of Talent Acquisition role, sourcing a diverse talent pool at mid-management levels, including executive management. She also acts as a consultative partner to her internal clients. As an HR professional, her goals are to help the company attract and hire stellar talent and bolster the pipeline of future candidates. Having a passion for the business of entertainment and media, Debbie tries her best to put the "HUMAN" back in Human Resources and act as a partner with the lines of business and internal clients she supports.

Debbie enjoys public speaking, mentoring, and volunteerism. She is a proud member of Alpha Kappa Alpha Sorority, Incorporated-NYC. Debbie has also sat on the Board of Candice's Sickle Cell Fund, Inc. (CSCF), a small non-profit raising awareness for Sickle Cell Disease, as well as an ongoing supporter of several non-profit organizations such as YMF, Inc. (The Yvonne McCalla Foundation), a breast cancer awareness non-profit, Gyrl Wonder, and Save a Girl, Save a World.

Debbie has used her voice on various platforms, such as Essence.com's 2020 Virtual Essence E-Suite: The Art of the Pivot series, NAMIC - National Association of Multi-Ethnicity in Communications, contributor to the PayScale.com article "How to Prepare for Your First Interview as a New Manager" June 2019, Google Digital Coaches, Harlem Digital Lab panelist on "How to Get the JOB - Tips and Tricks, Best Practices, Pre and Post Interview Advice, Job Search Tactics, and Interview Questions," New York Urban League - Women in Power: Lessons in Leadership panel, The New School–Milano Graduate School guest lecturer, Gyrl Wonder Leadership Academy workshop facilitator, The Future of Enterprise Podcast: "How to Curate Talent Strategies That Win, Engage, and Retain Talent," Circle of Change workshop facilitator, and many more!

Debbie received her MS in Human Resources Management from The Milano Graduate School of The New School University in New York and a BS in Social Work at SUNY-Stony Brook University, Long Island.

Follow Debbie for more updates from the "Talent Whisperer" at Debbie Douglas-LinkedIn or on Instagram at Debbie_Douglas18.

Resources

Job Search Checklist:
https://careerimprovement.club/blog/job-search-checklist-free-printable-pdf

5 Ways to Identify Your Perfect Employer:
https://www.careerhigher.co/career-advice/5-ways-to-identify-your-perfect-employer-1633/

Salary Negotiation Tips:
https://www.moneygeek.com/careers/resources/salary-negotiation

Debbie D. Douglas

Works Cited

David Cotriss (2023) Keep It Clean: Social Media Screenings Gain in Popularity Updated 1/23/2023 retrieved from https://www.businessnewsdaily.com/2377-social-media-hiring.html on February 7, 2023.

Alex Cavoulacos. [A Template for the Perfect Thank You Email After an Interview (Plus Samples!)] [original publication date. - N/A] [TheMuse.com] [Updated 8/12/2022.] [date of access-9-5-22.]

Vicky Oliver. 10 Common Job Interview Questions and How to Answer Them] [original publication date.11-11-21] [HBR.com] [date of access-9-5-22.]

Niki Jorgensen The Power of Social Media in Recruiting [publication date. 1-12-2023] Forbes.com, Forbes Human Resources Council [date of access-1-19-23]

Printed in the USA
CPSIA information can be obtained
at www.ICGtesting.com
LVHW011515020124
767837LV00030B/172